Contemporary
WEIGHT TRAINING

Contemporary
WEIGHT TRAINING

Jim Murray

Contemporary Books, Inc.
Chicago

Library of Congress Cataloging in Publication Data

Murray, Jim.
    Contemporary weight training.

    Includes index.
    1. Weight lifting.   2. Physical fitness.   I. Title.
GV546.M83   1978   796.4'1   77-91169
ISBN 0-8092-7550-3
ISBN 0-8092-7655-0 pbk.

Cover and exercise photos
posed by Fred Montero
and photographed by Don Prowant

Pen-and-ink illustrations
by Jay Murray

Published by Contemporary Books, Inc.
180 North Michigan Avenue, Chicago, Illinois 60601
Manufactured in the United States of America
Library of Congress Catalog Card Number: 77-91169
International Standard Book Number: 0-8092-7550-3 (cloth)
                       0-8092-7655-0 (paper)

Published simultaneously in Canada by
Beaverbooks
953 Dillingham Road
Pickering, Ontario L1W 1Z7
Canada

Contents

Introduction

If you want to increase your strength and/or improve the shape of your body, weight training is for you. Various forms of weight training are well established as the most effective way to build strength and power for rehabilitation, physical fitness, and athletic conditioning. Weight training is also unmatched for improving the body contours of both men and women. Furthermore, when done properly, weight training is one of the safest kinds of physically beneficial recreation.

The one drawback to weight training is that it is a relatively inefficient way to improve cardiovascular fitness and general endurance. When weight training is judiciously mixed with an activity such as jogging, rope jumping, cycling, or swimming, however, the blend provides everything the body needs in the way of exercise.

Weight training is a general term describing exercise in which the muscles are worked against fairly substantial resistance (although benefits can be obtained without straining against really heavy weights). It takes several forms.

One, which is properly called simply "weight training," is the subject of this book. Others are body building, Olympic lifting, and power lifting.

The basic equipment needed for weight training is a barbell, which consists of a strong steel bar, from five to seven feet long, with iron or steel collars that hold in place iron plates weighing from 1¼ to 50 pounds or more. Without the collars, these plates might either slip off the ends or slide in to the center where your hands grip the bar to lift it. (There are also barbells with plastic plates filled with sand, but iron plates are preferable because they take up less space on the bar.) Other important items of equipment are short steel bars onto which the plates can be loaded to make up dumbbells, one to be used in each hand. There also are exercise benches with upright supports to hold a barbell so that you can conveniently lie on a bench and perform supine presses (lifts you perform while on your back). And squat stands hold a barbell almost at shoulder height, from which you can take a heavily loaded barbell for leg exercises. These items of equipment are shown in illustrations throughout this book.

An adjustable barbell/dumbbell combination set that can be used as either a 15- to 100-pound barbell or a pair of 5- to 42½-pound dumbbells may cost from $40 to $60. A pressing bench costs about $40 and squat stands about $40 to $50 per pair. Additional iron plates cost about 40¢ to 60¢ per pound. Weights are among the best values in sporting goods and exercise equipment, since they never wear out.

One of the nice things about weight training is that you don't have to give it up as you get older, or if you become too busy to devote the hours needed for taking part in team games or competitive sports. Weight training can be continued, moderately, for a lifetime. It is an effective way to maintain muscle tone (and shape) even without exercising very hard. It can be done in very little time in the privacy of your home. A barbell set can be stored compactly in a garage, basement, or even under a bed, and is immediately available for 15 to 30 minutes of exercise at any time. Most people cannot even reach an athletic field or gymnasium in less than 15 minutes.

Myths about muscles

"Muscle turns to fat"

There are many misconceptions about weight training, and many self-appointed "experts" around who are prepared to expound on them. In every gathering there is someone who knew a fellow that developed gigantic muscles only to have them turn into massive blobs of fat when he quit exercising with weights. That's absolute nonsense. Muscle does not turn to fat.

Strong, well-developed muscles are likely to lose size if they are not exercised. And fat accumulates on most people who eat a lot and exercise little. But this has nothing specific to do with weight training. Many former athletes get fat when they give up their sport, regardless of the type of activity, if they take in more calories than they expend. And there are literally hordes of fat people who have never done much exercise of any kind.

"Exercising makes you muscle-bound"

Anyone who thinks weight training causes stiffness, clumsiness, slowness, or other adverse effects that might be described as "muscle-binding" should ask himself whether decathlon champions are muscle-bound. Weight training is used extensively by all top performers in this most demanding of all-around athletic tests. The decathlon demands speed, agility, power, strength, stamina, and diverse skills for running, jumping, hurdling, vaulting, and throwing. Yet such champions as Bruce Jenner, who set a world decathlon record at the 1976 Olympics, spend about a third of their training time working with weights. Jenner, who weighed less than 200 pounds, worked out with weights of well over 250 pounds on the barbell. It certainly didn't seem to handicap his versatile performance.

There is no intention here to imply that lifting weights and doing nothing else will produce decathlon champions. They must also train hard on running and especially must practice the skills of their ten track and field events. But weight training definitely is an asset to athletes, building strength and power that they can use effectively as long as they practice the techniques of their sports. The extent to which weight training will help an athlete depends upon the importance of strength and power in his sport. For example, it will help a football player or a wrestler more than it will a golfer or Frisbee player. But it will not handicap anyone who devotes adequate time to practicing whatever it is he or she wants to be skilled in.

"Weight training produces lumpy muscles"

Many people seem to believe that the inevitable result of weight training is the development of bulky muscles, wreathed with striations and liberally interlaced with prominent veins. This is because certain men with an aptitude for and intense dedication to body building with weights do develop such muscles.

Actually, very few people are of a physical type that can develop such muscles. Women can't, for the simple reason that one prerequisite for big muscles is an ample supply of male hormones, something that is lacking in normal women. The muscle and bone structure of most men also limits the extent to which they can pack on muscle.

Beyond physical aptitude, it takes hours of dedicated and very hard training to produce the kind of muscularity that wins Mr. America and Mr. Universe titles. The contest-winning body builders train as long and exhaustively as distance runners, with much greater intensity. In addition, they adhere to high-protein, low-carbohydrate diets that few people would be willing to stick to for very long.

Again, look at the decathlon champions. They exercise very hard with weights, but are not overly lumpy. In fact, most people would rate the physique of a decathlon champion as a masculine ideal.

As you progress with weight training, you will notice a definite improvement of muscle contours. In women, this will be manifested as curvier curves. In men, there will be some enlarging of muscles, but training can be kept at a maintenance level any time there seems to be danger that the muscles are getting "too big." Most men, whether they would admit it or not, would be delighted to have this happen!

"Weight training can cause hernia"

A person who is predisposed to hernia can get one from straining, and it certainly would be possible to overstrain while exercising with weights. But it isn't likely to happen, especially if a person exercises progressively, gradually building strength by first adding repetitions, then adding weight and then more repetitions, more weight, and so on.

Well-developed muscles actually protect against injury. A research physiologist, Dr. Peter Karpovich, obtained information on the incidence of injuries among 31,702 participants in weight training. He found that most injuries were relatively trivial, usually consisting of pulled muscles and tendons. These minor injuries were overcome by rest and then gradual resumption of activity. No heart injury was reported. And the incidence of hernia was found to be twenty times less than would have been expected among an average selection of people. (See *Weight Training in Athletics,* by J. Murray and P. V. Karpovich, Prentice-Hall, 1956.)

To practice weight training safely, you must learn correct body position (not to lift with a rounded back, for example). It is important for you to warm up by performing an exercise with a relatively light weight several times before moving on to weights that require greater effort. And keep the amount of weight to a level that you are sure you can handle, especially if you are exercising alone.

Weights, repetitions, and sets

In general, the way to practice weight training is to experiment with light weights, adding five or ten pounds at a time to the barbell. Practice the exercise a few times with each weight until you reach a weight that will not permit you to perform more than 5 to 8 repetitions without having to stop and rest.

When you repeat one exercise 8 times without resting, you have performed one *set* of 8 *repetitions* with a given amount of weight. In your next workout, you would do the same weight and repetitions, except that you should try to add 1 or 2 repetitions whenever 8 become easy.

When you can increase the repetitions to 12, it is time to increase the weight by five or ten pounds and begin the progression again at 8.

In addition to increasing the amount of weight, you can also build strength and improve proportions—and to some extent build endurance—by doing extra sets. For example, after doing 10 repetitions in one set you would rest a minute or two and do another set with the same weight, trying again for 10 repetitions. Then you would try it once more. A total of three sets is an effective approach in weight training, after you have become conditioned to the exercise. As your condition improves, the fitness-building effect of weight training is enhanced if you reduce the time of your rests between sets and exercises to a minute or less. (If you also are jogging or are active in some other aerobic activity, there is no need to make a special effort to shorten the rest periods between bouts of weight training exercise.)

For increased strength and improved body shape—which are the general effects of weight training—exercising in a range of 5 to 12 repetitions for three sets is an approach that works well for most people. An exception is that for problem areas such as excessive fat on the abdomen, it has been found effective to do more repetitions in specific exercises such as sit-ups and twists. Many learned exercise physiologists will insist that it is not possible to "spot reduce"—that is, to reduce fat more in one area of the body than in other areas. I'm sure there is scientific evidence to support the physiologists, but in practical experience it is possible to spot reduce by persistently exercising an area that is excessively fat. Part of the reduction results from improved muscle tone, which will make a waistline smaller even without loss of fat. But some of it comes from an actual loss of fat. Practicing a sustained, calorie-burning exercise such as jogging or walking will help a person lose fat. Simply taking a brisk half-hour walk daily will remove some excess fat for most people. A combination of walking or easy jogging and weight training and sensible diet will remove fat, increase strength, and improve both shape and cardiovascular fitness.

For more strength and power

For a greater and more rapid increase in strength, weight training can be done in several sets, increasing the weight and decreasing the repetitions with each set. This can be done most effectively with exercises that work major muscle groups, such as the supine press on bench and the squat (to be described later in this book). For example, suppose you can "bench press" 100 pounds 8 to 10 times for three sets and you decide you want to place more emphasis on increasing strength. Instead of doing 10, you might do only 8 repetitions with 90 pounds to warm up and then increase the weight to 110 or 120 and do 5 or 6; increase again to 120 or 130 and do 3 to 5; and increase again to 130 or 140 and do as many as possible, perhaps 1 to 3. Then you would drop back to 100 pounds for 8 to 10. With this system, every time you can do 5 repetitions with the heaviest weight on the final set while working up, you add ten pounds at each step in the whole series and begin the progression again. When working up in this manner, especially in the bench press and squat exercises, you should work out with a training partner who can help you if you should overestimate yourself on a given day and get stuck in the down position with either lift.

Recommended numbers of sets and repetitions are given in this book with the descriptions of individual exercises. In each case you will need to experiment to determine the amount of weight needed to give you an adequate workout for the number of repetitions suggested.

In summary, three sets of 5 to 12 repetitions is a good general approach to weight training for increasing strength and improving shape. To place more emphasis on strength and power, do sets of 8-6-4-2 with increasing weights and then a final set of 8 to 10, dropping back to about as much weight as you used for the first set of 8. The weight training exercises should be done three days a week, with non-training days intervening between training days. For example, you might work with the weights on Monday, Wednesday, and Friday, or on Tuesday, Thursday, and Saturday. The off days provide time for your body to recover and build more strength so that you will be able to handle more weight, or the same weight more easily, in subsequent workouts.

For all-around fitness

If you are seeking all-around general fitness, you should either walk briskly, jog, ride a bicycle, skip rope, or swim two or three of the days when you are not involved in weight training. Half an hour of walking or cycling at a steady, not-too-leisurely pace, or 10 to 20 minutes of jogging or rope skipping two or three days per week will burn excess calories and provide cardiovascular benefits. Serious athletes, of course, would need to follow an intensified running program, including half a mile to a mile of jogging plus some faster running at shorter distances. They would also need to strive for heavier poundages in weight training, with an approach emphasizing strength and power on alternate days.

In this photo, Fred Montero is set to press the barbell overhead. (Photo by Don Prowant.)

1

What you can expect from weight training

Anyone can expect increased strength, improved appearance, and a sense of well-being from regular practice of weight training.

This assumes, however, that the exerciser is in normal health to begin with. If in doubt about your readiness to begin an exercise program of any kind, you should see your physician. Tell him or her what you plan to do and have a checkup if the doctor believes one is needed. If your doctor says anyone who exercises is silly, however, try another doctor. Some doctors know more about sickness than they do about health.

Power lifting

Beyond the small improvements that anyone can expect from a moderate investment of time and energy, the ultimate possibilities of strength and power that can be achieved with weight training are best expressed in weight-lifting competition. One form of competition makes use of basic training movements—squat, bench press, and dead lift—conducted under controlled conditions and with specific rules detailing methods of performance. This competition is called power lifting, though it is really more a test of grinding strength

Figure 1.1   The dead lift

In the dead-weight lift or "dead lift," one of the three power tests, the lifter must stand erect with the weight, as shown. Several heavyweights and super heavyweights have raised more than 800 pounds in the dead lift.

than explosive power. The heaviest weights, as might be expected, are lifted by big men, athletes standing 5'10" or more and weighing from 240 to more than 300 pounds.

Such giants of strength as Jim Williams, Don Reinhoudt, Jon Kuc, and Doug Young have actually bench pressed 600 pounds and more. Reinhoudt, Kuc, and Jon Cole (who has also won the United States discus-throwing championship) have dead lifted in the range of 800 to 900 pounds and have squatted with comparable weights. The all-time champ in squatting has to be Paul Anderson, however, the 5'10", 300-pounds-plus Georgia strong man who squatted with 1,200 pounds (that's *one thousand, two hundred pounds!*).

Olympic lifting

In Olympic weight lifting, two lifts are contested. These are the snatch and the clean and jerk.

In the snatch, the barbell must be pulled from the floor to fully straightened arms overhead in a single, unbroken motion. The lifter is permitted to lower himself under the weight, either by splitting (lunging) with one leg forward and the other back or by squatting. The squat is more efficient. Some of the world's best lifters at body weights of 240 pounds to 300 and over have snatched more than 400 pounds with this method.

The second Olympic lift is the clean and jerk. In this lift, the barbell must be pulled from the floor to the chest in a distinct movement (the "clean") and then must be shoved overhead with a second effort, no pause being permitted except while the lifter gathers his resources after the clean. Most champions squat to catch the weight on their chests in the clean, and then split one leg forward and the other back to lower themselves under the ascending barbell in the jerk.

In both the Olympic lifts, the competitor must hold the weight overhead under control to the satisfaction of the referee before the lift is considered good. The heaviest

Figure 1.2.   The squat clean

Dropping into a squat position for the clean, as shown,
enables competing Olympic lifters to lift (or "clean") heavy
weights to their chests. They must then rise and jerk the
barbell overhead.

weights are lifted overhead by big men weighing from 240 to
more than 300 pounds. A gigantic Russian, Vasily Alexeyev,
standing over six feet tall and weighing approximately 350
pounds, achieved two great milestones in weight lifting when
in 1970 he became the first to clean and jerk 500 pounds and
then a few years later was the first to succeed with 550
pounds. There is no comparable feat in sports. It is as if the

Figure 1.3. The jerk

In jerking a weight overhead, Olympic lifters are permitted to
split (lunge) under the weight to help them get it to straight-
arm position, but they must finish by bringing their feet into
line and holding the weight overhead under control.

first man to pole-vault 18 feet also became the first to go
over 19 feet or the first 70-foot shot-putter were to move on
to 80 feet.

Actually, smaller athletes are relatively better lifters.
The possibilities of strength relative to size are shown by

such men as David Rigert, 5'9½" tall and 198 pounds, who snatched approximately 200 pounds more than his own weight and cleaned and jerked almost 300 pounds more than his body weight. The best power lifters relative to size squat with 400 to 500 pounds more than they weigh, bench press 300 to 350 pounds more than they weigh, and dead lift 400 to 500 pounds more than body weight.

Lifting for conditioning

Unless you have aptitude for lifting, however, it is unrealistic to think of trying to compete with champions.

The popular television show "Superstars" showed that topflight athletes, including many who trained with weights as part of their conditioning programs, could jerk weights overhead only half as heavy as those lifted by the best Olympic lifters. Many world-class athletes in very demanding sports could not jerk 200 pounds overhead. Some strong and well-built athletes managed 200 to 250 pounds, but only physical giants—champion shot-putters and professional football players—were able to lift from 250 to 300 pounds overhead. And these were all athletes who used some weight training for conditioning.

The same is true of the exercise lifts. Whereas world-champion power lifters in the 242-pound class squat with more than 700 pounds and bench press in the 500- to 600-pound range, I have known successful professional football players, very strong men and superior athletes weighing around 250 pounds, who trained very hard with weights during the off-season, to reach bench presses in the 300- to 400-pound range and squats to bench level with 400 to 500 pounds. Many fine collegiate football players and wrestlers have been strong enough for their demanding sports when they achieved bench presses of 20 to 80 pounds over body weight and squats of 50 to 150 pounds more than they weighed. From this perspective, a bench press of body weight or a bit more and a squat with 50 pounds more than body weight become creditable feats of strength for a person using weight training to maintain strength and muscle tone, and to contribute to physical fitness.

The bench press is the best all-around upper body exercise.

2

Upper body exercises

Building the chest muscles

One of the most effective chest-building exercises—the supine press on bench—is actually the best single overall upper body exercise. It also affects the shoulders, arms, and to some extent the upper part of the latissimus muscles that impart width to the back. (These back muscles are affected because they are tensed to help control the weight, not because they help in the lift to any great extent.)

The reason the supine press—called the bench press—is so effective is that relatively heavy weights can be used in the exercise. Suppose, for example, you could do 10 curls with 70 pounds and 10 standing presses with 100 pounds. A comparable amount of weight for the bench press would be 120 to perhaps 150 pounds.

To practice the bench press, you need a sturdy bench, preferably one that has supports near the head end where you can place the barbell and load it, and from which you can take the barbell at straight arms to begin pressing. If you don't have such a bench, you'll need a willing training partner to pick up the barbell and hand it to you. If you are going to try heavy weights or a limit number of repetitions, you should always have a partner standing by as a "spotter," to help you get the weight up if you are unable to press it. The potential danger that you could get stuck with a heavy weight resting on your chest is obvious.

The exercise is done as follows: Using an overhand grip, take the barbell at straight arms over your chest, hands about 25 to 30 inches apart (this is somewhat wider than you would use in pressing overhead). Lower the weight smoothly, under control, to touch the lower part of your chest (pectoral) muscles and immediately push it back up to straight arms. Keep your elbows out to the sides while pressing.

Do three sets of 8 to 12 "reps" (repetitions) or, if you want more rapid increase in strength, do 8-6-4-2, adding about 10 pounds per set, and then drop back to approximately the starting weight and do 8 to 12 reps. When you begin to develop superior strength and can bench press at least 200 pounds once or twice, the increases per set are larger: for example, do 135 pounds for 8 reps, 165 for 6, 185 for 4, and 200 for 2; then go back to 135 for 10 to 12 reps.

Very heavy weights can be lifted in the bench press if you are ambitious. No athlete in a vigorous sport should be satisfied with a personal record for the bench press of less than equal his own weight. A lift of 50 pounds more than body weight is within the reach of any athlete who isn't handicapped by unusually poor leverage. Most husky college football players can bench press 250 to 300 pounds and many pro football linemen can bench press from 300 to 400. A few do even more, as do most world-class shot-putters and discus throwers. The 1968 Olympic decathlon champion, Bill Toomey, weighing only 190, could bench press more than 300 pounds.

The bench press can also be done with dumbbells,

Figure 2.1.   The bench press
with barbell

The bench press permits use
of heavy weights and is the
best all-around upper body
builder, affecting chest, arms,
and shoulders.

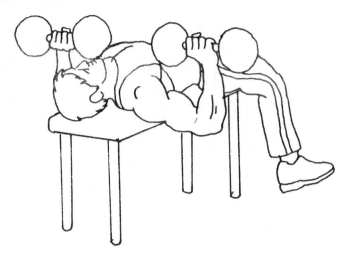

Figure 2.2.   The bench press with dumbbells

Bench pressing with dumbbells stretches the chest (pectoral) muscles more than when the exercise is done with a barbell.

though considerably less total weight can be used than with a barbell. A variation is to set a sturdy board at about 45 degrees (making sure it is braced so it won't slip or fall sideways) and do bench presses while leaning at an angle (called incline presses). Special benches for incline presses are available at most gymnasiums. The exercise can be done with two dumbbells or a barbell for three sets of 8 to 12 reps. In the incline press, the weight is pressed straight up but the angle forces the upper part of the pectoral muscles to do most of the work.

The flying exercise

An especially effective exercise for the chest muscles is called flying, because its motion is like the movement of a bird's wings except that it's done in a supine position. The

Figure 2.3.   The incline press

Pressing from an inclined position exercises the upper part of
the chest muscles as well as the shoulders and arms.

exercise is actually a bent-arm lateral raise done on a bench.
You hold two dumbbells directly over your chest, palms
inward; bend your arms slightly and lower the dumbbells out
to the sides as far as possible, stretching your chest muscles
fully; and then contract your chest muscles to bring the
dumbbells back to the starting point. In most exercises,
nature will tell you when to breathe (before making the

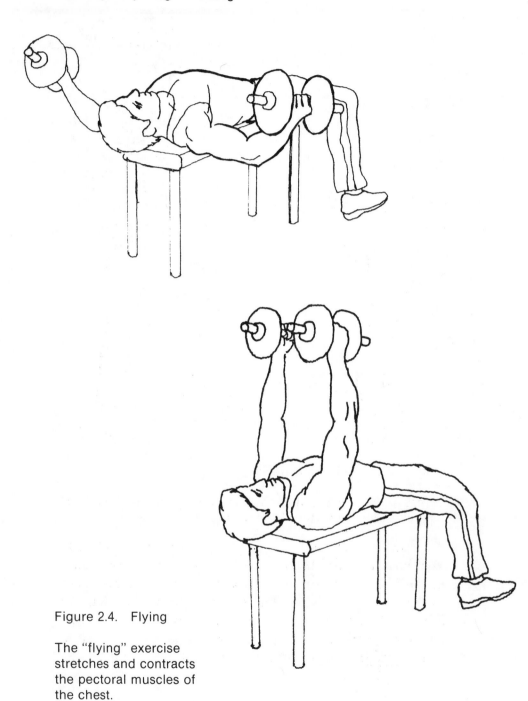

Figure 2.4.   Flying

The "flying" exercise
stretches and contracts
the pectoral muscles of
the chest.

effort), but in the flying exercise it's a good idea to consciously breathe in as you lower the weights to the sides and breathe out as you raise them.

Another chest-building exercise done with conscious attention to breathing is the pullover. For this you might use either light dumbbells, a single dumbbell held with both hands, a light barbell held with a close grip, or a dumbbell bar with plates loaded in the center, held at the ends with both hands. (When using a single dumbbell for this exercise, you should hold it with hands around the handle and overlapping against the plate at the end, so that the other end of the dumbbell hangs down.) In all of these exercise variations, you lie either on a bench or across one. Starting with the weight held directly over your chest, you lower it with arms almost straight as far behind your head as it will comfortably go. As you lower the weight, you inhale steadily so that your lungs are full just before the weight reaches the lowest point. Then you pull it forward again over your chest, exhaling. Do 10 to 15 repetitions, three sets. This exercise is often done after a set of squats, a leg exercise that produces a feeling of breathlessness, since the pullover aids recovery and seems especially effective when there is a natural demand for deep breathing to repay the oxygen debt incurred during exercise. The exercise develops muscles of the chest and upper back, but is intended mostly to stretch and enlarge the rib cage.

A variation of the pullover that has a good muscle-building effect on the chest and upper back is done with arms bent. You lie on a bench with your head hanging over the end. Grasp a barbell resting on the floor, using a fairly narrow grip (hands about 6 to 12 inches apart), and—keeping your arms bent at about a right angle—pull the weight up over your face to your upper chest. Lower it and repeat. Do 8 to 12 reps, three sets.

Building the back muscles

One of the best exercises for the latissimus dorsi—the

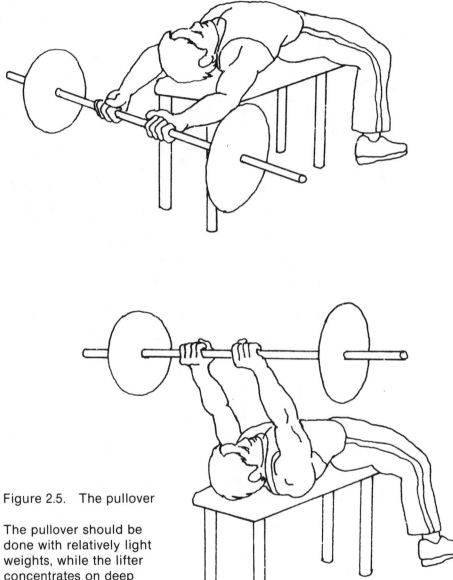

Figure 2.5.   The pullover

The pullover should be done with relatively light weights, while the lifter concentrates on deep breathing to stretch the rib cage.

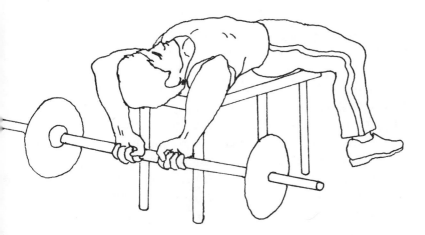

Figure 2.6.   The pullover
with arms bent

Bent-arm pullovers, as shown, build
both chest and upper back muscles.

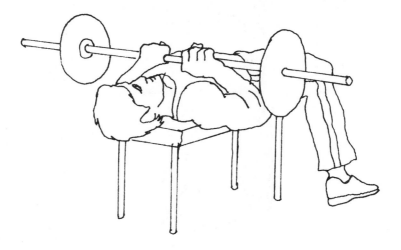

muscles that run from under the arms to the waist and, when well developed, give the back a V shape—is the old-fashioned chin-up. The latissimus muscles pull the arms down and back, which is what you do when chinning. If you have a chinning bar, practice the exercise with both an underhand and an overhand grip, and with hands spaced both wide and narrow. If you are strong enough, three sets of 8 to 12 reps will make chinning effective in developing your upper back.

One disadvantage of chinning is that you must be able to haul your own weight up each time. If you have access to a gymnasium with a "lat machine"—an overhead pulley with a handle attached to adjustable weights—you can do the chinning motion to the chest and to the back of your neck with lighter weights. This is a great asset to beginners.

Figure 2.7. Chinning

Old-fashioned pull-ups exercise the latissimus dorsi, the muscles that broaden the back.

Even without special equipment, however, there is an excellent upper back exercise that you can do with a barbell. It's called the bent-over rowing motion and is done like this: Grasp a barbell with an overhand grip, hands spaced about shoulder width. Lean forward from the hips, keeping your head up and your back as flat as possible, approximately parallel with the floor. Keep your knees slightly bent to

Figure 2.8.   The bent-over rowing motion

The rowing motion, leaning forward, is the best overall upper back exercise.

Figure 2.9. The hyperextension

Hyperextensions start with a
forward bend and finish with a
strong upward arching motion.

relieve strain on your lower back and the backs of your legs.
In this position, pull the barbell from where it hangs directly
below your shoulders until it touches the upper part of your
abdomen. Continue for 8 to 12 reps, three sets.

The upper back muscles are impressive looking and are
important in such sports as crew (rowing) and wrestling, but
the lower back muscles that run along on either side of the

spine are perhaps more important in terms of function and long-term fitness. A direct exercise for the lower back is the hyperextension, which requires either a special apparatus found in well-equipped gyms or the assistance of a training partner. With a training partner to anchor your feet, you lie prone (face down) across or along a bench so that your thighs are supported but your upper body extends past the bench and is unsupported. In this position, you perform a sort of inverted sit-up with hands clasped behind your head. Lower your head and torso so that your forehead almost touches the floor and then arch upward as high as you can. Begin this exercise without resistance. Then, as soon as you can do a dozen hyperextensions without difficulty, hold a light barbell plate behind your head. The weight should be heavy enough to restrict you to about 8 reps. Work up from 8 to 12 before adding weight, doing up to three sets.

A simpler exercise for the lower back is the dead lift. In this one, you stand close to a barbell, bend down and grip it with hands about shoulder width apart, and smoothly stand up with it until the weight is across your thighs. You can hold the bar more easily in the dead lift if you turn one palm forward (underhand) and the other back (overhand). You should keep your head up and your back as flat as possible while doing this exercise. And start with your legs well bent, so that your hips are lower than your shoulders throughout the lift. Do three sets of 5 to 10 repetitions. Heavy weights can be handled in the dead lift, as long as you keep your hips lower than your shoulders and your back flat. It is possible to lift 200 to 500 pounds or more in this way, but progression should be gradual and cautious.

A variation of the dead lift is done with straight legs and has even more effect on the lower back muscles than the regular dead lift. This lift must be done with caution, however, with a very deliberate bending and straightening, to avoid straining the lower back muscles and ligaments. In the stiff-legged dead lift, you should use much less weight than in

Figure 2.10.   The regular dead lift

The regular dead lift strengthens back and grip. Reversing the hands helps the lifter hold a heavy barbell.

Figure 2.11.   The dead lift
            with legs straight

The stiff-legged dead lift,
which is like toe-touching
with a barbell in the hands,
strengthens the back and
makes it flexible.

23

the regular dead lift, since the leverage places great stress on a vulnerable area when you lift with your legs straight. Do three sets of 10 in the stiff-legged dead lift, increasing the weight only when it feels *very* light and easy to lift. For most people, 100 to 150 pounds will be plenty to use in this exercise, even after months of training. Fifty pounds should be enough for a beginner.

To strengthen the trapezius muscles, which run from the neck out to the shoulders, pick up a barbell as in the dead lift and then shrug your shoulders as high as possible, attempting to touch your shoulders to your ears. Do three sets of 8 to 12 reps.

One of the best back exercises—in fact, one of the best strengtheners and conditioners of the total body—is the power clean. In this exercise, you stand close to the barbell, ankles almost touching it, and crouch to grasp it with an

Figure 2.12. The shrug

When the lifter performs shrugs with weights, the shoulders should be drawn up toward the ears as high as possible.

Figure 2.13. The power clean

The barbell clean (power clean) begins with a leg and body extension, arms hanging straight, and then finishes with a strong arm pull from thigh level to get the weight chest-high. Note the straight back position during the pull.

overhand grip. Pay particular attention to starting with your hips lower than your shoulders and with your back flat (the back *must not* be rounded). Begin to lift by extending (straightening) your legs, letting your arms hang straight. As the extension of your legs and body raises the weight past knee height, begin to pull with your arms, keeping the barbell close to your thighs and body, accelerating it upward. Pull as high as you can with your elbows up, fully extending your legs and body, and then whip your elbows down and forward, turning the barbell over to catch it at your chest. Bend your knees to lessen the impact as the barbell turns over and strikes your chest. Lower the weight carefully, under control, either to the floor or to just above knee height, and repeat 5 reps, 3 to 4 sets. This is a difficult exercise, requiring coordination and timing, but it is also a great movement for building explosive power and total strength, affecting the legs, back, shoulders, and grip. If you can do this exercise five times with 100 pounds you're not doing badly, but good athletes work up to single power cleans with body weight

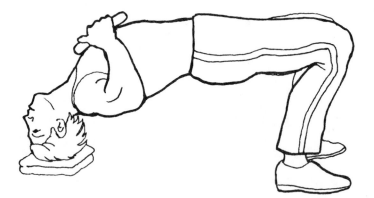

Figure 2.14. The wrestler's bridge

The wrestler's bridge, is unexcelled for developing the neck muscles, especially with added weight on the chest.

and more. John Petersen, Olympic wrestling champion, did eight repetitions with 255 pounds!

It pays to learn the power clean because this is the correct way to lift a barbell to your shoulders, preparatory to pressing it overhead.

The next exercise isn't really for the back, but it does develop neck muscles that tie in with the trapezius. It's called the wrestler's bridge and is the best single neck exercise. To perform it, you need a mat or a folded towel or sweatshirt to form a pad. Place the pad on the floor and lie with the back of your head on the near edge of the pad. Pull your feet up close to your buttocks and arch up, digging your head into the pad so your weight is supported on your feet and head. Arch high, so you roll on your head from the back to the forehead and then down again. Repeat in sets of 5 to 8 at first and work up to 12. Then hold a light barbell plate on your chest and begin again at 5 to 8 reps, gradually increasing to 12. This exercise is especially helpful to wrestlers and football players, who should continue to work up until they can do the exercise with 25 to 50 pounds of weight.

The barbell curl, a basic biceps-builder, is demonstrated by Fred Montero. (Photo by Don Prowant.)

3

Arm and shoulder exercises

Curls for the biceps and forearms

The single best, most basic exercise for developing the biceps muscles of the upper arms, along the front of the arm from elbow to shoulder, is the curl. This can be done with a barbell or with dumbbells. It can also be done with other types of resistance apparatuses, such as pulleys, but this requires access to a gymnasium or health club.

First is the barbell curl. Grasp the barbell with an underhand grip (thumbs outward and palms away), keeping your hands spaced about shoulder width. Stand with the barbell resting across your thighs, arms hanging straight, and then flex your arms—keeping your elbows at your sides—and bring the barbell in an arc to your upper chest. Lower smoothly, resisting as the weight goes down, and repeat. Do a total of 8 to 10 repetitions (reps) and work up to three sets. Try to increase the number of reps in each set. When you can easily do 12, 10, and 10, increase the weight enough to restrict the reps to 8 and begin the progression again.

Figure 3.1.   The barbell curl

The barbell curl, with palms up, builds strength and size in the biceps of the arms.

A good goal for men is to gain strength enough to curl 60 to 70 pounds for 10 to 12 reps. If you can do 100 pounds for 10 reps (smoothly, without heaving or swinging the weight up), you are very strong. Exceptionally strong body builders (men with arms that measure 18 inches around or more) can do the curl for 10 reps with 150 pounds.

Curling with dumbbells

Curling two dumbbells is another very good way to develop the biceps. One reason dumbbells are especially

Figure 3.2. Curling two dumbbells

In curling, the dumbbells are turned as illustrated. The palms are almost touching the front of the shoulders at the finish.

effective is that you must do an equal amount of work with each arm and cannot shift part of the weight to your stronger, better-coordinated arm as you can with a barbell. Another advantage of dumbbells is that they allow you to rotate your hands as the weight is curled and this enhances the contraction of the biceps muscles. Do dumbbell curls like this: Stand with a dumbbell in each hand, arms hanging naturally at your sides with palms in. Flex your arms, bringing the dumbbells up in arcs to your shoulders, and rotate your palms up (so your thumbs are pointing outward) as you raise the weights. Lower and repeat, working up with three sets of 8 to 12 reps.

You would not ordinarily do both barbell and dumbbell curls in the same workout, unless you were specializing in body building. But there is a dumbbell curl, working one arm at a time, that you might want to add after doing either the barbell or two-dumbbells curl. This is the "concentration curl," done as follows: Either seated or standing, lean forward so that one arm hangs free, holding a dumbbell. With deliberate effort, concentrate on contracting the biceps muscle and bring the dumbbell to your shoulder. Work in the range of 8 to 12 reps for three sets, alternating arms. You should use less weight in this exercise than in the regular curl, since the emphasis should be on contracting the muscle rather than on handling more weight. Some exercisers prefer to brace the elbow of the arm that's working against the inside of the thigh to prevent swinging the dumbbell and to help them focus the effort.

A variation of the barbell curl, called the reverse curl, is done with an overhand grip, knuckles away and thumbs toward the center of the barbell. This is done like the regular barbell curl, with the exception that your hands are in the overgrip. Reverse curls make the forearm muscles work harder and prevent the biceps from working as efficiently as they do when you use an undergrip, so you can't use as much

Figure 3.3.   The
             concentration
             curl

Concentration curls, shown
here, focus exercise on the
biceps.

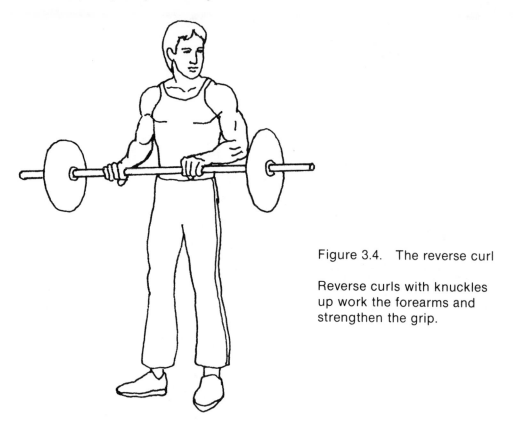

Figure 3.4. The reverse curl

Reverse curls with knuckles up work the forearms and strengthen the grip.

weight in this exercise as in the regular curl. With three sets of 8 to 12 reps, it's a great exercise for strengthening the forearm muscles that increase your gripping power.

For even more direct forearm exercises, do the "wrist curl." In this one you sit, holding a light barbell or two dumbbells, with your forearms supported by your thighs and your hands extending past your knees. In this position, raise and lower the weight by moving your hands and wrists only. Get as much range of motion as possible. Repeat three sets of 10 to 15 reps with palms up and three sets of 10 to 15 with palms down.

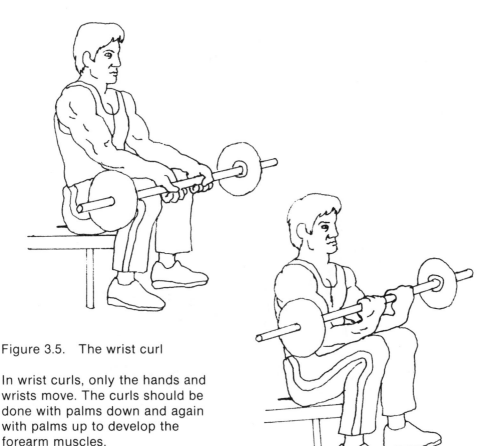

Figure 3.5.   The wrist curl

In wrist curls, only the hands and
wrists move. The curls should be
done with palms down and again
with palms up to develop the
forearm muscles.

Exercises for the triceps

The triceps muscle of the back part of the arm is much
larger than the biceps and is brought into play whenever you
extend (straighten) your arm. The best way to develop the
triceps is to perform exercises that concentrate effort on that

Figure 3.6   The triceps extension,
                         standing

Triceps extensions, with elbows
kept pointing upward, work the
backs of the arms.

muscle alone. Three variations of arm extension exercises are especially effective.

One is the triceps extension, standing, also called the "French Press." Hold a light barbell with an overgrip, hands fairly close together (thumbs inward, about 8 to 12 inches apart), and lift it straight overhead. Then, keeping your elbows pointing straight up, lower the barbell in an arc to the back of your neck and force it up overhead again. Nothing should move except your forearms, with your elbows continuing to point straight up and acting as a hinge for the movement. This exercise, done for three sets of 8 to 12 reps, both stretches and contracts the triceps. The first time you do it, you will know what muscles have been worked, because the triceps will feel sore a day later. Work the soreness out by doing the same exercise with a light weight until you can do a full 12 repetitions in good form. Then increase the weight and begin the progression again at 8 reps.

A variation is to do the same exercise while lying supine. In this form of triceps extension, you hold the barbell with an overgrip, hands no more than 12 inches apart, and lower it (carefully!) to touch your forehead lightly, or a point just behind the head. Then force the barbell back up, keeping your elbows high. In the supine position, you can make the exercise more effective by keeping your elbows tilted back slightly (toward your head) throughout the exercise. This maintains tension throughout. Do three sets of 8 to 12.

If you are doing triceps extensions standing, you likely will not want to do them in the supine position during the same workout, unless you are specializing in body building. But you might want to give the triceps some extra work after one or the other of the extensions by doing the "kickback." In this exercise, you lean forward with one arm braced below, holding a fairly lightweight dumbbell in the other hand. Bring the arm holding the dumbbell alongside

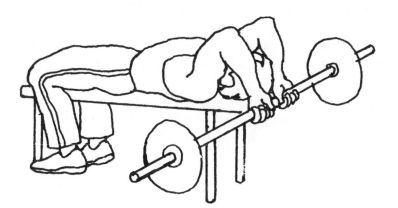

Figure 3.7. The triceps extension, supine

Triceps extensions, lying supine, can be done from behind the
head, as shown, or from the forehead. The muscles get added
work when the upper arms are tilted slightly toward the head.

Figure 3.8.   The triceps kickback

The triceps kickback calls for
backward extension of the upper
arm, keeping it level, and then a
slight extra raise of the dumbbell
with the arm straight.

your body and hold the dumbbell at your shoulder, as though
you had just curled with it. Then, keeping your upper arm
along the line of your body, approximately horizontal as you
lean, force the dumbbell back and up in an arc, allowing
your upper arm to rise slightly at full extension in order to
fully contract the triceps muscle. When you do this right,
you can feel a slight cramping of the triceps. Work your
arms alternately with three sets of 8 to 12 reps for each.

The overhead press

Another of the key basic exercises, one that strongly involves both the deltoid muscles that cap the shoulders and the triceps, is the overhead press, with barbell or two dumbbells. With a barbell, you take an overhand grip, hands spaced slightly wider than your shoulders, and lift the barbell to your upper chest. From a position where the barbell rests against your collarbone and the front of your shoulders, push it smoothly past your face to the point at which your arms are fully locked directly overhead. The moment your arms reach full lock, bend them again and lower the barbell to touch your chest. Continue in this manner for 8 to 12 reps, three sets.

A variation on the overhead press is to do one press as described and then lower the barbell to touch low at the back of your neck for subsequent repetitions. You need a somewhat wider grip to do presses behind the neck. If you are doing regular presses with your hands 22 inches apart, for example, you may need to space them 24 to as much as 28 inches apart in order to lower the barbell comfortably behind your neck. You will also need to use somewhat less weight when pressing behind the neck.

Still another variation is to press with two dumbbells, holding them so that the handles point straight out from your ears and the plates or spheres on the ends touch the outsides of your shoulders at the beginning of the press. An advantage in training with dumbbells is that you must work each arm and shoulder equally hard. The difficulty of controlling two separate weights, however, will limit the total amount of weight you use to less than you could press with a barbell, and probably less than you could press behind the neck.

Ten presses with a 100-pound barbell or two 40-pound dumbbells is good; 10 with 150 pounds on the barbell is very good; and any number of presses with 200 pounds or more would rate in the super-strong category.

Figure 3.9.   The overhead press
with barbell

The barbell press, straight up
overhead, is one of the best
exercises for developing the
shoulders.

Figure 3.10.   The overhead press
with dumbbells

The dumbbell press starts with
arms well to the sides and
finishes with arms pointing straight
up. The palms are kept forward
throughout.

The three types of presses would not ordinarily be done in the same workout, except by an ambitious body builder preparing for a best-built-man contest. In the final chapter of this book we consider how the exercises can be organized into comprehensive exercise programs.

The upright rowing motion

Another basic shoulder-builder (one that also strongly affects the trapezius muscles running from the back of your neck out to the shoulders) is the upright rowing motion. For this one, you grasp the barbell with an overhand grip, hands only a few inches to no more than a foot apart. Then, standing with your arms hanging straight, barbell across your thighs, you pull the barbell up to your throat or chin, keeping your elbows higher than the barbell throughout the exercise. Lower and repeat for a total of 8 to 12 reps, three sets.

The lateral raise

Although the presses and the upright row are exercises for shoulders and arms combined, there are exercises that can be done with dumbbells that strongly focus on the three sections of the deltoid muscles without too much involvement of surrounding muscle groups. The most basic of these is the lateral raise. Do it like this: Hold a lightweight dumbbell in each hand, arms hanging at your sides, with knuckles out (thumbs forward). Then, keeping your arms nearly straight, raise the dumbbells sideways until they are higher than your shoulders—at about ear level. While raising the dumbbells, keep your knuckles up; that is, don't allow your thumbs to point upward. In fact, it's an even more effective exercise for the sides of your shoulders if you keep the dumbbells tilted slightly downward at the front end. Do three sets of 8 to 12 reps. The lateral raise is a leverage

Figure 3.11.   The upright rowing
motion

In the upright rowing exercise, the
elbows are kept higher than the
barbell throughout.

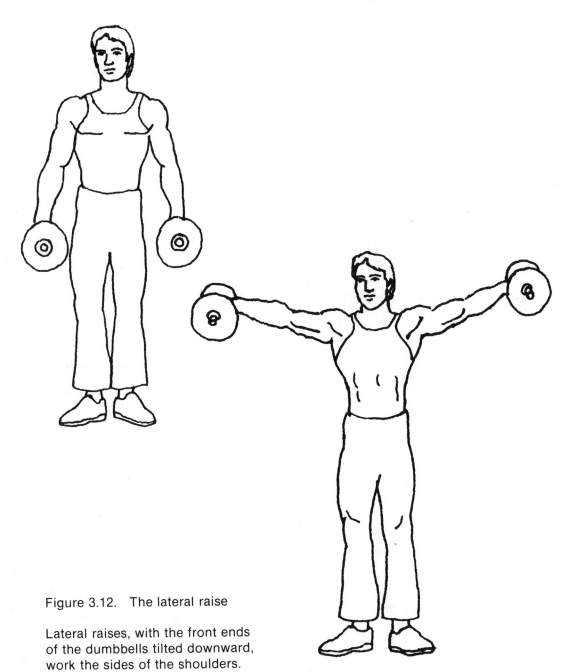

Figure 3.12.   The lateral raise

Lateral raises, with the front ends
of the dumbbells tilted downward,
work the sides of the shoulders.

exercise. The fact that you keep your arms almost straight makes it difficult for anyone but exceptionally strong men to do the exercise correctly with much more than 10- to 20-pound dumbbells.

The lateral raise develops the sides of the shoulders. The various presses develop the entire shoulder area, but mostly the front part of the deltoid muscle. If you feel you need extra work for the front part, a good exercise is the alternate

Figure 3.13.   The alternate forward raise

Alternate forward raises, with dumbbells, work the anterior (front) deltoid muscles.

forward raise with dumbbells. For this one you stand with the dumbbells across the fronts of your thighs, arms hanging straight. Then raise one dumbbell straight in front of you, all the way up overhead. Lower the first dumbbell and raise the second one simultaneously so that they pass each other directly in front of your shoulders. Continue for 8 to 12 reps with each arm, three sets.

All the exercises for the shoulders described so far affect the front and sides of the deltoid muscles, but have minimal effect on the rear part at the back of the shoulder. To get at the back part, you must do the lateral raise exercise while leaning well forward, at an angle of 45 to 90 degrees. While leaning forward, again keeping your arms almost straight, you raise a pair of dumbbells simultaneously to the sides (which, because you're leaning, is backward) as high as you can. Do three sets of 8 to 12 reps.

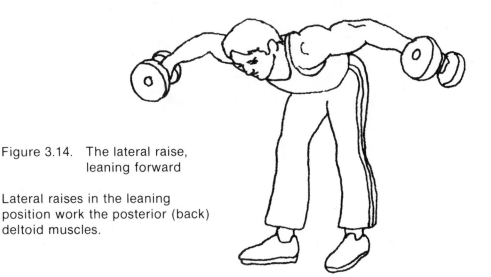

Figure 3.14.   The lateral raise,
                  leaning forward

Lateral raises in the leaning
position work the posterior (back)
deltoid muscles.

Fred Montero demonstrates correct position for the squat, with torso erect, back slightly arched *(not rounded)*, and legs bent to the parallel level. (Photo by Don Prowant.)

4

Developing the legs

Barbell exercises

The essential basic exercise for the legs is the squat with a barbell across your shoulders. This exercise strengthens the legs and also makes the whole body strong. It is essential for football players and weight men in track and field (shot-putters, and discus and hammer throwers) and for anyone who wants to gain solid body weight.

To do the squat properly, you need stands to place the barbell on, from which you take it at shoulder height to begin the exercise. If you don't have stands, you will need two training partners to help you get the weight in place, especially if you train seriously on the exercise and eventually work up to using 200 pounds or more. With the barbell on stands and loaded to the desired weight, place your hands fairly far apart on the bar and duck under it so that it is centered across your upper back and shoulders just below the back of your neck. (Many exercisers roll a folded towel

Figure 4.1.   The squat with barbell
on shoulders

No exercise is more effective for
strengthening the legs than the squat
with a barbell on the shoulders. Note
that the back is kept straight, not
rounded.

around the bar for padding.) Lift the barbell off the stands and step back one or two steps to be clear of the uprights. Place your feet a comfortable distance apart, about hip width, with toes pointing slightly outward. Take a breath high in your chest and, keeping an upright position with your back flat, sink with a controlled effort until your legs are bent at approximately a right angle. Rise immediately and exhale. Inhale, squat again, and continue for a total of 8 to 12 reps. Work up to three sets of 12, 10, and 10 before adding weight and beginning the progression again.

The squat is another exercise in which you can build great strength by doing 8-6-4-2 reps with increasingly heavy weights and then a final lighter set of 8 to 12 with about as much weight as you used for the first set. For example, suppose you could achieve a "limit effort" of 2 reps with 200 pounds for the squat. You would start with 135 pounds for 8 reps, then do 165 for 6, 185 for 4, 200 for 2, and return to 135 for 10 to 12 reps. Whenever you could add a repetition with the heavier weights, you would add five pounds all along the line except for the first set. A warmup with 135 is heavy enough for anyone, even an advanced athlete who will work up to 300 or 400 pounds. If you find it hard to judge when you are low enough in the squat, try placing a bench or box behind you that comes just to the height of the tops of your calf muscles where the lower leg attaches to the knee. Squat just deep enough to touch the bench lightly.

A variation of the squat is to do the exercise while holding the barbell across your upper chest and shoulders in front of your neck. The leverage is unfavorable when you do front squats, so you will not be able to use as much weight as when you hold the weight across the back of your shoulders. It may help you maintain correct position (erect, with flat back) if you place a board one or two inches thick under your heels. The thigh muscles closer to the knees will get an especially good workout if you elevate your heels on a two-inch-thick board, keep your feet only six to ten inches apart,

Figure 4.2.   The squat with barbell in front

Front squats cause the lower thigh, near the knee, to work especially hard. Note the straight back.

and point your toes straight ahead (and maintain a very erect position).

Incidentally, some exercise physiologists believe it over-stretches the structure of the knees to allow the thighs to go any deeper in the squat than to a point just below parallel with the floor. That is, you would not go any lower than a position with the tops of your thighs horizontal. For a body-building effect, however, better results are obtained by going somewhat lower. Many experienced weight trainers do not believe this does any harm to the knees as long as the exercise is done with a smoothly controlled effort—with no bouncing in the low position.

To exercise the muscles of the lower legs, the calves, take a weight on your shoulders as though to do squats. Stand with your toes and the balls of your feet elevated on a board

Figure 4.3.   The rise-on-toes,
             or calf raise

The rise-on-toes should be done on a
block or board to stretch the calf
muscles as well as contract them.

one or two inches thick. Rise as high as you can on your toes; then lower until your heels are fully stretched to touch the floor, and repeat. Do 10 to 15 reps and work up to three sets. To work the calf muscles thoroughly, do the exercise three ways: with your feet pointed straight ahead, with toes turned out (heels in), and with toes pointed inward (heels out).

A variation of the rise-on-toes exercise is useful if the

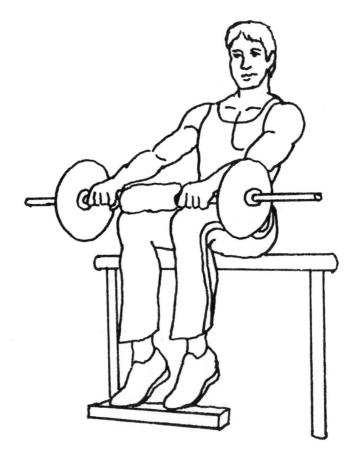

Figure 4.4.   The rise-on-toes, seated

The rise-on-toes in a seated position develops the lower portion of the calf muscle.

lower calf is underdeveloped, or if it responds poorly to the exercise when done as described. Try doing the exercise seated, with the barbell (thickly padded) resting across your thighs near your knees. Again, do three sets of 10 to 15 reps, changing foot position for each set.

Exercises with special equipment

Two other very good leg exercises, the leg curl and the leg extension, require access to special gym equipment or the use of weighted exercise sandals called "iron boots." These are available in sporting-goods stores or by mail order from such firms as the York Barbell Company, the Weider Barbell Company, Iron Man Barbell Company, and the Lurie Barbell Company. Such home exercise equipment is advertised in the following magazines, available on newsstands: *Strength & Health, Muscular Development, Muscle Builder/Power, Iron Man, Muscle Training Illustrated,* and *Muscle Mag International.*

Using an iron boot with dumbbell attached (the metal sandals are designed to hold a dumbbell bar), you can develop the thigh biceps (large hamstrings) by standing on a box or thick board so the foot with the weight is clear of the floor, then flexing the weighted leg until the knee is bent past a right angle. Do 8 to 12 of these leg curls, three sets, working first one leg and then the other, alternately. The use of a slant board, firmly braced, allows you to do the exercise more conveniently than you can while standing. Lie against the board with your head at the high end (and hold on), and perform the leg curls in this position. With a slant board you may be able to work both legs at a time.

A special apparatus with pulleys is available for doing leg curls in most gyms. This equipment makes it much more convenient to do the exercise.

The leg extension exercise also can be done with an iron boot and dumbbell. In this one, you sit on a sturdy bench or table that is high enough to let your legs dangle without

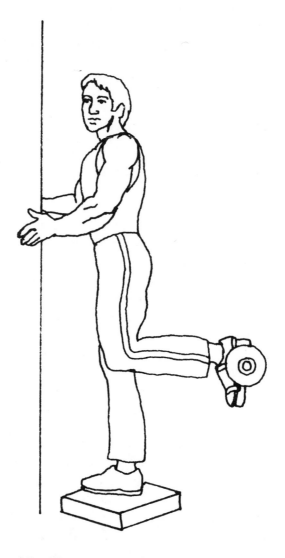

Figure 4.5.   The leg curl

The thigh biceps can be exercised by doing leg curls with a dumbbell attached to an "iron boot," a metal sandal designed to hold a dumbbell bar.

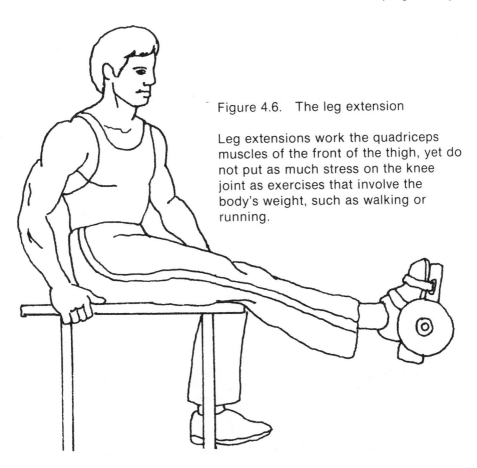

Figure 4.6. The leg extension

Leg extensions work the quadriceps
muscles of the front of the thigh, yet do
not put as much stress on the knee
joint as exercises that involve the
body's weight, such as walking or
running.

touching the floor. Sitting so that your thigh is supported to
the knee, extend the foot with the weight until your leg is
straight. Lower your foot and continue for a total of 8 to 12
reps. Exercise both legs, alternately. This exercise is especially good for strengthening the quadriceps—the front thigh
muscles that stabilize the knee. It can be used for rehabilitation after injury, as soon as the exercise can be done without
pain—though a doctor should be consulted about this if there
has been any damage to the joint.

Hip and thigh exercises for women

The squat, leg curl, leg extension, and calf raise (rise-on-toes) are all good exercises for women, to improve leg shape and increase firmness or for athletic conditioning. Many women need additional exercise for their hips and upper thighs, however. Two of the best such exercises are kicks to the side and to the back.

For the side kick, lie on your right side and raise your left leg sideways as high as possible 5 or more times, gradually increasing repetitions to 20. Repeat the exercise with the right leg, lying on your left side. This tones the side of the upper thigh and the side of the hip.

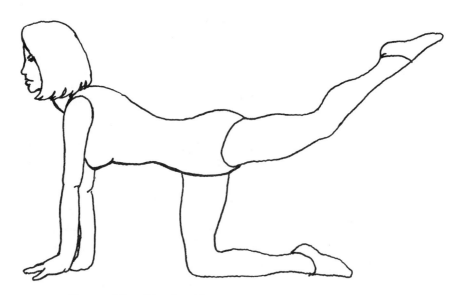

Figure 4.7.   The back kick

High back kicks, from a position down on all fours, are effective hip toners for women. The knee should be brought to the chest and then the leg should be extended as shown. For trim hips, the exerciser also should kick sideways while lying first on one side and then the other.

The back kick is an effective exercise for the backs of the hips (the buttocks). To do the back kick, assume a position on all fours, as though to crawl. Then draw the right knee up toward your abdomen as tightly as possible and push it back straight to full extension, raising your foot high behind you. Work up from 5 or more repetitions to 20 with each leg.

The back kicks and the side kicks can be done in sets if the hip area is really flabby and in need of considerable firming. Three sets are probably enough with each leg.

The knees should be bent and feet anchored for sit-ups.

5

Exercises for a trim midsection

To firm and trim the midsection, there are four basic exercises that affect the front of the abdomen and the sides, just above the hips. These are the sit-up, the leg raise, the side bend, and the twist.

In Chapter 2 we described two exercises for the back that also help greatly in trimming the torso: the hyperextension and the power clean. Walking and jogging are also excellent exercises for trimming the midsection.

The sit-up

The most direct basic exercise for the front of the abdomen is the sit-up, done as follows: Lie supine with your feet under a supporting object (or held down by a training partner) and knees bent. Clasp your hands behind your head, take a breath, and *exhale*, drawing your abdomen in as much as possible. As you draw your abdomen in, bring your chin toward your chest and "crunch up" into a sit-up, touching

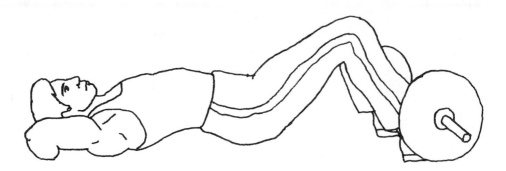

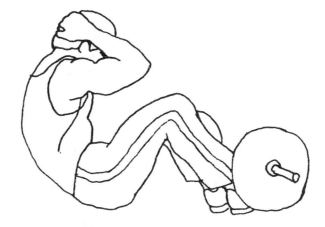

Figure 5.1.   The sit-up

Sit-ups should be done with knees bent to relax leg and hip muscles and focus the work on the abdominal muscles.

your elbows to your knees. Return to the supine position and continue for a total of 10 to 20 repetitions.

Don't rush through the sit-ups. Breathe in and out, sucking in your abdomen with each sit-up. It may help you contract the abdominal muscles if you will also consciously tilt your pelvis up slightly at the start of the sit-up.

When you can easily do three sets of 20 sit-ups, hold a five-pound weight behind your head and begin the progression again, working up to three sets of 20 and then moving up to use a 10-pound weight behind your head. Or, if sit-ups are easy for you, continue to 50 sit-ups in a single set.

The leg raise

Another good exercise for the abdominal muscles is the leg raise, done as follows: Lie on an exercise bench, holding on to the bench near your head or with hands braced alongside your hips, with your feet and legs extended, touching the floor. Allowing your knees to bend slightly, bring your legs up until your feet are directly over your body. Lower and repeat for a total of 10 leg raises. As in the sit-up, consciously try to draw your abdomen in as you make the effort. Add repetitions to 20 or more and continue to three sets of 20 or a single set of 50. The exercise can be done on an inclined bench to increase the degree of difficulty.

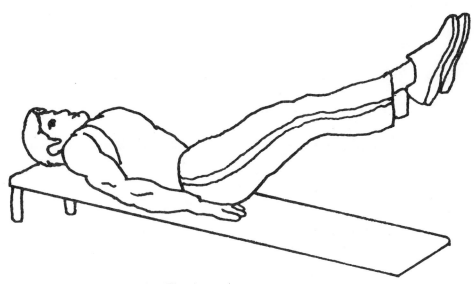

Figure 5.2. The leg raise

Leg raises exercise the abdominal muscles, especially the lower portion.

Figure 5.3.   The side bend

Side bends, which involve leaning to one side and then
returning past a vertical position, strengthen the muscles
along the sides of the waist.

The side bend and the twist

To firm the muscles of the sides, stand with one arm
hanging at your side, holding a single dumbbell. Place the
other hand behind your head. Lean toward the side where
you are holding the dumbbell, and try to reach your knee
with the dumbbell. Then straighten and continue past a

vertical position, leaning away from the hand holding the dumbbell. Repeat these side bends for 10 to 20 reps on each side, working up to three sets.

Another good exercise to tone the sides is the twist. In this, you hold an unloaded barbell across your shoulders behind your head, sit on a bench, and twist around as far as you can go to the right and then to the left. Do a total of 20 to 50 reps. If you don't seem to get results from twists while sitting, try doing them while standing and bending forward from the hips.

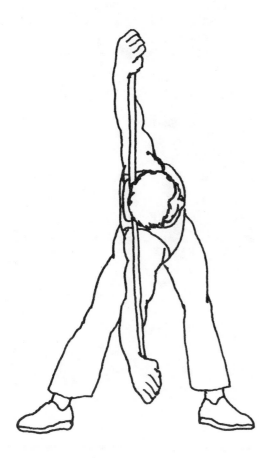

Figure 5.4.   The twist,
standing

Twists, leaning forward, are effective for working the sides and trimming the waist.

Completion of the regular overhead press, an excellent shoulder and arm exercise, is shown by Fred Montero. (Photo by Don Prowant.)

6

Getting it all together

We've considered basic exercises for every part of the body. Now it's time to think about how these exercises are put together for a balanced workout.

First, please note that I haven't described every possible exercise that can be done. I've deliberately kept to fundamentals that you can practice on your own with a minimal investment in equipment. For more detailed information, a good source is my book *Inside Weight Lifting and Weight Training*. Or, if you want specific information on body building, you'll find it in a more comprehensive book I've written on that subject entitled *Inside Bodybuilding*. And Franco Columbu, winner of Mr. Olympia and Mr. Universe titles, has prepared a book called *Winning Bodybuilding*. These three books are available from Contemporary Books, Inc., which published this basic book.

Planning a complete workout

In planning a workout that will make use of the basic

exercises, consider what you're trying to accomplish. If you are seeking general strength, improved fitness, and better appearance, the following workout will do the job. For total fitness, do this routine three days a week and jog for 10 to 15 minutes on two or three of the days when you don't do weight training.

1. Warm up by taking a lightweight barbell and dead lifting it several times, cleaning it to the shoulders several times, and pressing it overhead several times 22,25
2. Sit-ups, 20–50 repetitions
3. Barbell curl, three sets, 8–12 reps 30
4. One-arm concentration curl, one to three sets, 8–12 reps, each arm 33
5. Barbell press, three sets, 8–12 reps 41
6. Triceps extension, standing, two or three sets, 8–12 reps 36
7. Lateral raise, three sets, 8–12 reps 45
8. Bench press, three sets, 8–12 reps 11
9. Flying exercise, one to three sets, 8–12 reps 14
10. Rowing exercise, two or three sets, 8–12 reps 19,44
11. Hyperextension, two or three sets, 8–12 reps 20
12. Squat, three sets, 8–12 reps 50
    [alternated with]
13. Pullover, 10–15 reps, after each set of squats 16
14. Rise-on-toes, 15–20 reps, one to three sets 53
15. Repeat favorite exercise, one to three sets, or select an exercise for weakest body part, one to three sets

For greater power and strength—which might be your goal, for example, in an off-season athletic conditioning program—the following workout is recommended:

1. Warm up with lightweight dead lifts, cleans, and overhead presses

2. Sit-ups, 20 reps, using enough weight behind head to make 20 reps difficult
3. Power clean, decreasing reps 5-5-3-3-2-1-1, increasing the weight with each set as you decrease the reps
4. Bench press, decreasing reps 5-5-5-3-3-2-2-1, increasing the weight as you decrease the reps and then dropping back to a weight you can press for 8-10 reps
5. Squat, decreasing reps 5-5-5-5-3-3-1-1, starting light and increasing the weight as you decrease the reps
6. Rowing motion, 8-10 reps, two to three sets
7. Dumbbell curl, 8-10 reps, two to three sets
8. Dumbbell press, 8-10 reps, two to three sets
9. Lateral raise, 8-12 reps, two to three sets

If the power program is part of athletic conditioning, you should run on two or three days when you are not weight training. A general approach is to jog half a mile and run a series of shorter distances (perhaps 220s) at about three-fourths your best speed, keeping rest periods between runs to a minimum—about two to three minutes of walking. Shorter sprints—40 to 50 yards—with quick starts are important also for football players.

Women would exercise with a slightly different emphasis. The following offers a good general approach:

1. Sit-ups, 10-20 reps
2. To firm arms: curl, 10-12 reps; triceps extension, 10-12 reps
3. Leg raises, 10-20 reps
4. For sides: twists, 20-50 reps
5. For bust and arms: bench press, 10-12 reps; flying exercise, 10-12 reps, three sets
6. Kicks to rear, on all fours, 10-20 reps, each leg

    7. Kicks to side, 10–20 reps, each leg
    8. Squat, 8–12 reps, one to three sets
    9. Rise-on-toes, 10–15 reps, one to three sets
  10. Pullover, 10–15 reps, one to three sets

If overweight, women should walk, jog, or cycle two or three days per week in addition to the weight training. Walking or cycling should be for 20 minutes to half an hour; jogging, for 10 to 20 minutes.

Selecting repetitions and weights

Note that repetitions are recommended usually within a range of, say, 8 to 12, and that no weight is suggested. Each individual must experiment to find the amount of weight that feels right for the prescribed number of reps.

The lower you keep the number of reps, assuming that the weight is heavy enough to make the last couple of reps difficult, the more strength you build. For great power, it's necessary to work with enough weight so that you can't do more than 3 to 5 reps. This is why it is necessary to increase the weight with each set while reducing the number of repetitions. For general muscle toning, shape, and strength, the range of 8 to 12 is effective; but you must be guided by how you feel and your own ambition.

It is fruitless to try to do more repetitions or increase the weight if you feel "stale"—listless and sluggish. On such an off day, it's better to reduce either the weight, the number of repetitions, or the number of sets—or some of each.

Selecting exercises

The sample routines listed in this chapter do not include all the exercises, but rather include one or two good exercises for each body part. After you exercise for a while, you may become bored with doing the same exercises time after time. Then you should substitute other exercises for the same body part. For example, change from barbell curls to dumbbell curls and from standing triceps extensions to supine triceps extensions. Do the power clean instead of the hyperextension and leg raises instead of sit-ups. Switch from the regular squat to the front squat.

It's also all right to add exercises, but it would be too much if you were to do all the exercises described in this book in one workout.

If you want to emphasize trimming the midsection, you could do the 14 exercises suggested for a general workout and then add leg raises, side bends, and twists. Or you could do one of these waistline exercises after each of the other exercises: for example, sit-ups, curls, leg raises, presses, twists, lateral raises, sit-ups again, bench presses, leg raises again, rowing exercise, twists again, and so on.

If you want to emphasize arm development, you might add reverse curls or dumbbell curls to the barbell curl and concentration curl. And you might add the triceps kickback after the triceps extension.

As you practice weight training, it is a good idea to keep a training diary, writing down the routine that you are following and recording changes in weights and numbers of reps as you progress. Once you have established a solid routine that provides ample exercise for the body parts you want to improve, stick with it for at least four to six weeks. Many beginners make the mistake of changing routines with almost every workout, or of adding exercises almost randomly. This is not productive. To progress, you must emphasize solid basic routines and work hard at them.

It would be better to select half a dozen basic exercises and plug away at them than to do all the exercises shown in this book in one workout. For example, three to five sets of power cleans, bench presses, curls, presses, and rowing—and one set of sit-ups—would produce good results if practiced regularly three times a week. A more diversified routine is better, but only if you apply yourself to it diligently. A variety of exercises is given in this book to help you relieve boredom by modifying your routines, but don't confuse boredom with impatience. Stick with a routine long enough to give it a chance to work.

On the other hand, after six weeks or so on the same routine it is a good idea to make a change—always taking care to include an exercise for each body part and being sure not to neglect exercises that you need just because you happen to like some of the other exercises better. The caricature of a weight-trained man is familiar in real life as well as in cartoons: with big arms, shoulders, and chest from curling and bench pressing—and with scrawny legs from neglecting exercises that aren't as much fun.

As you experiment with exercise routines—giving each one enough time for a fair evaluation—note in your training diary how you felt about your response to the exercises as well as your training poundages. Referring to your notes will help you go back later to the more productive routines. It also will help you select effective portions of routines to be combined into an overall program that ultimately may prove best for your individual physical and psychological makeup.

Another important point: Don't hesitate to take an easy workout on occasion. You will find that you are not able, physically and psychologically, to to push yourself always to equal or exceed your previous best effort. If you try too hard, you may find yourself retrogressing because you are "stale"—literally overtrained.

Two important things to remember are these: (1) Include at least one exercise for each body part, and (2) Don't do too many exercises for any one body part. That's a little like saying, "Train hard, but not too hard." It seems obvious, but it's important. Knowing what is enough but not too much is something you have to learn for yourself, by trial and error.

Diet and rest

A person who wants to be physically fit, and especially a man who wants to increase strength and muscle size, must obtain an adequate balanced diet of natural foods. Essential nutrients are obtained from the following:

> Eggs, meat, poultry, fish, and legumes for protein and minerals
> Leafy green vegetables and yellow vegetables, for vitamins and minerals
> Citrus fruits, tomatoes, raw cabbage, and salad greens, for vitamin C and roughage
> Potatoes and similar root foods, and fruits, for starch, vitamins, and minerals
> Milk and milk products (cheese, cottage cheese) for calcium and protein
> Cereals and bread for energy, vitamins, iron, and minerals
> Butter and margarine or vegetable oil for vitamin A and oil

Athletes in hard training and anyone who wants to gain strength and size will need more food than sedentary people do. A good way to obtain the needed nutrients is to eat small amounts several times a day rather than one or two big meals. Ample protein, in particular, is needed to build muscle size and strength, though fats and carbohydrates also are required for the energy that is burned in a workout.

Food supplements are popular with many top athletes and body builders. Among the most popular are vitamin C with bioflavinoids, desiccated liver tablets, and vitamin E in the form of wheat germ oil. Protein supplements, especially those with high-quality essential amino acids (from egg and milk sources), are also popular. Anyone in doubt about the balance of nutrition supplied by his or her diet might be well advised to take a supplement containing multiple vitamins and minerals.

Adequate rest is also important for anyone expecting to build strength and size with weight training. People's need for sleep varies, but an average is probably 7 to 8 hours out of a 24-hour day. Beyond that, however, a person seeking to build strength should not engage in continuous physical activity between training sessions. A day or two free of strenuous activity is essential during a building phase. Common sense will tell you that your body can rebuild itself better after a workout if you take in a movie and get eight hours of sleep than if you spend four or five hours dancing at a disco and sleep only five or six hours.

Sources of up-to-date information

If you get really serious about weight training, you will find the following magazines to be good sources of current information: *Strength & Health* and *Muscular Development*, both published at Box 1707, York, Pennsylvania 17405; *Muscle Builder/Power*, 21100 Erwin Street, Woodland Hills, California 91364; *Muscle Mag International*, Unit One—270 Rutherford Road, Brampton, Ontario, Canada; *Iron Man*, 512 Black Hills Avenue, Alliance, Nebraska 69301; and *Muscle Training Illustrated*, 1665 Utica Avenue, Brooklyn, New York 11234. These publications are available at newsstands as well.

Glossary

Aerobic activity—an activity that continues for relatively extended periods of time, ten minutes or more, causing deeper and faster breathing and an increased heart rate (to a rate approximately double the resting rate for people in their late teens to thirties), yet at an intensity low enough that it can be continued without causing great discomfort or forcing the exerciser to stop and rest. Easy jogging, fast walking, and continuous bicycling are among the most popular aerobic activities among exercise enthusiasts.

Athletic conditioning—a system of exercises done to prepare an athlete generally, and especially to participate effectively in a sport. Weight training, as described in this book, is used in athletic conditioning to increase strength, power, size, and muscular endurance. Running is used to increase general endurance and cardiovascular fitness as a part of athletic conditioning.

Bar—a bar is a steel handle used in weight training. A bar may be little more than a foot long for use as a dumbbell handle to more than seven feet long for use in weight-lifting competition.

The weight of a dumbbell bar may be as little as 2½ pounds (which must be counted, along with weights that are placed on it). The heavy competition (Olympic) bars weigh 20 kilograms (44 pounds) or 45 pounds. Most bars for exercise barbells are five to six feet long and weigh 15 to 25 pounds. Bars are 1¹/10 inches in diameter.

Barbell—basic weight-training equipment, consisting of a steel handle (the bar), usually five, six, or seven feet long; weighted metal plates (disc-shaped, with holes in the center to fit on the handle) used to vary the amount lifted; and collars fixed to the handle (usually with screws) to keep the plates from sliding along the handle.

Bench—an essential accessory in weight training, because a bench is used in several key exercises. The best exercise benches are those with upright supports on which a barbell can be placed for bench presses. Benches without supports, both flat and inclined, are used for a variety of exercises in gymnasiums.

Bench press—probably the single best upper body exercise, working the arms, shoulders, and chest as the barbell is pushed up and down from chest to straight arms while the exerciser lies supine on a bench. The term also refers to a competitive lift in which the competitor gets three attempts to make his single best effort. The bench press is a good test of upper body strength, though leverage is involved as well. *See also* **Power lifting.**

Calorie—a measure of the energy value of food. It takes, roughly, 15 calories per pound of body weight per day to maintain a person's size (allowing for considerable variation in individuals). If more calories are taken in as food and drink than are used up by activity, the body stores some of the excess as fat. If insufficient calories are taken in to provide fuel for a person's activity, the body uses up stored fat.

Carbohydrates—high-energy nutrients contained in high-calorie foods, which are readily stored by the body as fat. Physical fitness enthusiasts try to obtain carbohydrates from fruits and vegetables rather than from refined sugar and flour, although these are also sources of carbohydrates.

Figure G.1.   Bench press

The bench press is one of three tests of strength in power lift competition. Some of the strongest super heavyweights (over 242 pounds) have lifted 600 pounds and more in the bench press.

Cardiovascular fitness—the body's ability to perform sustained work or very brief, demanding work, without adverse effects or great discomfort from the effort. Cardiovascular fitness (or cardio-respiratory endurance) is improved by regular jogging, or by brief bouts of more intense exercise interrupted by relatively short rest periods. Since much of the stress in exercise is placed on the heart (and does not harm a healthy heart), it is a sensible precaution for a person beginning an exercise program to have a medical examination to be sure there are no physiological restrictions on vigorous activity.

Clean and jerk—competitive lift in Olympic weight lifting, the clean and jerk is a test in which the heaviest poundages are hoisted overhead. There are two distinct parts to the lift. First is the "clean," which is a pull that raises the barbell from the floor to the lifter's chest. Second is the "jerk," in which a coordinated thrust powered by the legs and arms shoves the barbell overhead where it must be held under control.

Collar—a small, circular piece of metal with an integral screw or other tightening device that fits over a barbell handle. The outside diameter of a collar is larger than the diameter of the hole in the barbell plate. Collars are placed at equal distances from the ends of the barbell and fastened in place to leave anywhere from three to a little more than four feet of bar as gripping area for the exerciser or lifter. After plates are placed on the bar, another pair of collars is placed on, (outside the weights), to keep them from slipping off.

Cycling—riding a bicycle, either a regular bicycle that is made for outdoor travel or a stationary exercise cycle in a gymnasium; a good form of aerobic exercise that contributes to cardiovascular fitness.

Dead lift—a competitive lift in "power" contests and an exercise that is used to develop the strength of the back and the grip in particular. The lifter crouches and grasps the barbell (usually with one hand in an overgrip and the other in an undergrip), then stands smoothly erect, finishing in a position with his shoulders back, head up, and the barbell hanging at straight arms across the upper thighs. *See also* **Power lifting.**

Decathlon—the decathlon is a ten-event track and field test of all-around athletic ability in diverse types of skills calling for speed, strength, power, and endurance. It includes the 100-meter dash, long jump, shot put, high jump, 400-meter run, 110-meter hurdles, discus throw, pole vault, javelin throw, and 1,500-meter run. Decathlon champions use weight training to build strength and power, which is perhaps the best evidence that such training does not cause a person to become clumsy, slow, or "muscle-bound."

Dumbbell—a short-handled barbell, to be used in one hand. Dumbbells are available as cast-iron balls or squares permanently attached by short steel handles; as molded plastic filled with sand; or as short steel handles with plates and collars so the amount of weight can be varied for different exercises.

Endurance—there are two major types of endurance, cardiorespiratory and muscular. Cardiorespiratory endurance refers to the ability of the heart, lungs, and blood vessels to supply oxygen to working muscles so the body can function at a relatively high level for a sustained period of time. Muscular endurance is the ability of the muscle fibers to contract repeatedly or to sustain a single contraction for a long time.

Fitness—*see* **Physical fitness.**

Jerk—*see* **Clean and jerk.**

Jogging—a form of slow, easy running, considered one of the best kinds of exercise to improve cardiovascular fitness. Many exercise physiologists believe the way to improve cardiovascular fitness is to jog at a pace that will require your heart to beat at 70 percent of its maximum for at least 10 to 20 minutes. Maximum heart rate varies with age. A rate of approximately 140 equals 70 percent of maximum at age 20-25, 136 at age 30, 128 at 45, 124 at 50, 110 at 55, and 111 at 60. Obviously, a beginner should jog moderately and gradually increase to the recommended ten minutes or more.

Mr. America—a title awarded annually to a man who has outstanding muscular development and definition, and whose body is well proportioned and symmetrical. This is a major national contest in the United States, open to men who have won other best-built-man contests such as Mr. New York City, Mr. California, or Mr. Central States.

Mr. Universe—a title awarded annually for muscular development, definition, proportions, and symmetry on an international (and presumably interplanetary) level, open to winners of national best-built-man contests. Beyond Mr. Universe is the Mr. Olympia contest, a professional best-built-man competition open to winners of major international contests.

Muscle-bound—a term applied to a person with well-developed muscles who happens to be slow and/or clumsy. By contrast, if a thin, fat, or average person is slow or clumsy, that person is just referred to as not very fast or not very well coordinated.

Muscularity—a condition in which muscles are well developed and are covered by very little fat, so that the shape and definition of individual muscles are evident.

Olympic lifting—two lifts—the snatch and the clean and jerk—performed in Olympic competition. Contests involving the same two lifts are also held in state, district, national, and international meets the world over on a regular basis. In the snatch, a barbell must be pulled from the floor to a position overhead with arms fully straightened in one motion. In the clean and jerk, a barbell must be pulled from the floor to the chest in one motion (the clean) and then, in a second motion (the jerk), rammed to fully straightened arms overhead. The lifter may squat or split (lunge) under the weights to assist himself in getting them to his chest or overhead, but he must finish standing erect with the barbell overhead under control. The man who lifts the most total weight in the snatch and the clean and jerk is the winner. There are weight classes in Olympic lifting, with the following limits: 114½ pounds (52 kilograms), 123½ lb. (56 kg.), 132¼ lb. (60 kg.), 148¾ lb. (67½ kg.), 165¼ lb. (75 kg.), 181¾ lb. (82½ kg.), 198¼ lb. (90 kg.), 220½ lb. (100 kg.), 242½ lb. (110 kg.), and unlimited (over 242½ lb.). A 165-pound lifter could receive an Olympic lifting classification (IV) by snatching 135 pounds and cleaning and jerking 185 for a total of 320. To reach the highest classification (Elite, good enough to contend for a world championship) he would have to snatch 270 and clean and jerk 350, or make some other combination on the two lifts that would add up to 620.

Physical fitness—a state of being in which an individual is free of disease (or has chronic disorders under control) and is capable of sustained exertion without undue fatigue or discomfort or of brief, powerful effort without sustaining injury.

For example, a person who without physical penalty could run a mile in eight minutes and bench press a barbell equal to his body weight would have both endurance and strength, and thus would be called physically fit.

Plates—in weight training, flat discs of varying sizes (thickness and diameter) with holes through their centers that allow them to be slipped onto the ends of bars to make up barbells or dumbbells of varying weights. Plates may be of cast iron or semisteel, or of plastic, filled with sand. Plates are manufactured in weights of 1¼, 2½, 5, 7½, 10, 12½, 15, 20, 25, 35, 45, 50, 55, 75, and 100 pounds (and in comparable metric weights).

Figure G.2. Power lifting: squat

In power lifting, the squat tests leg and general body strength. The athlete is required to bend his legs until the tops of the thighs are slightly lower than parallel with the floor. Several super heavyweights have squatted with more than 900 pounds.

Power—the ability to exert great muscular strength very quickly. Power—strength with speed—is the quality needed to jerk a heavy barbell overhead. Power is also needed to sprint, jump, or throw well in track and field competition.

Power lifting—actually a misnomer; a form of weight-lifting competition in which the contestants strive to lift the greatest total amount of weight in three events: the squat, bench press, and dead lift. These events are tests of power to some extent, because the lifters do move as fast as they can, but the nature of the lifts and the extreme heaviness of the weights lifted make them a test more of sheer strength (with technique, of course) than of explosive power. Power lifting has the same weight classes as Olympic lifting. To reach class IV in power lifting, a 165-pound man would have to achieve a total of 810 pounds, which he might do by squatting with 280, bench pressing 200, and dead lifting 330. To be classified Elite he would have to total 1,480 pounds, which he might do by squatting with 520, bench pressing 380, and dead lifting 580.

Press—to push a barbell or dumbbells to straight arms overhead. *See* **Bench press.**

Proteins—body-building nutrients found in eggs, milk and milk products (cheese), and lean meats. Proteins are also found in most other foods, but the best sources—eggs, milk, meat—contain a complete protein that is readily used by the normal body to build muscle.

Repetitions—in weight training, the number of times a given exercise is repeated without stopping to rest. Because weight training is performed in series of repetitions, or "reps," with the muscles alternately relaxing and then contracting fully, it is an isotonic exercise rather than—as is often erroneously stated—an isometric exercise. (In isometric exercise, the exerciser strains against an immovable object so the muscles tense but do not shorten as in isotonic exercise.)

Resistance—in weight training, the amount of weight the muscles are worked against in performing an exercise. The principle of weight training—also called "progressive resistance exercise" in rehabilitation work—is to gradually increase the resistance from workout to workout so that the muscles are able to adapt to the challenge and become stronger.

Rope skipping—jumping over a swinging rope that is held by the jumper (usually with handles), one end in each hand, as it swings over the head and under the feet; one of the very best cardiovascular conditioning exercises. Rope jumping (or skipping) for ten minutes continuously is an excellent way to achieve and maintain aerobic fitness if practiced at least three days per week.

Sets—in weight training, the completion of a given number of "reps" (repetitions) in an exercise. If you curl a barbell 10 reps, that makes "one set of 10." If you curl it 10 reps, then rest; curl it 10 more reps, rest; and curl it 10 reps again, you have done three sets of 10.

Snatch—the first of the Olympic lifts (the other is the clean and jerk). In the snatch, a lifter must pull a barbell from the floor to fully straightened arms overhead in a single, unbroken motion. He may squat or split (lunge) to lower himself under the weight as it goes up, to help him get it all the way up in one motion; but he must then rise and hold the barbell overhead under control for the lift to be complete. A snatch with a barbell equal to the lifter's weight is very good, but the best international-caliber lifters snatch from 100 to approximately 200 pounds more than they weigh.

Squat—in weight training, a lifter does the basic squatting exercise by holding a barbell across the back of his shoulders and sinking with controlled strength until his thighs are approximately parallel with the floor and then rising again for a given number of repetitions, usually between 5 and 12. In power lifting, a competitor has three tries to lift his maximum weight in the squat in single efforts. He is required to bend his legs until the tops of the thighs are parallel with the floor and then to rise again until his legs are straight. *See also* **Power lifting.**

Squat stands—twin supports on which a barbell can be placed a bit

Figure G.3. Snatch

In the snatch, one of the two Olympic lifts, the lifter may squat under the weight as shown, to get it to arm's length above his head in one unbroken pull. He must then rise and hold the weight overhead under control.

lower than shoulder height and then loaded with weights for performing squats as an exercise or in competition. The stands are also used for other exercises in which the exerciser wants to take the weight at that height. For example, an Olympic lifter will use stands to shoulder a barbell for practicing jerks overhead. The best squat stands, which cost about $40 to $50 or more for a pair, are adjustable to accommodate people of different heights.

Strength—the ability to overcome resistance by muscular effort.

Supplement—in weight training, specially formulated nutrients used to increase the intake of protein or vitamins, or some other food component believed useful in building strength and/or health. Supplements are usually in tablet, powder, or liquid form.

Swimming—steady swimming is an aerobic exercise comparable in its effect on the cardiovascular system to jogging, running, cycling, or fast walking.

Vitamins—essential elements in nutrition that enable the body to make proper use of its food intake to maintain health. Vitamins believed especially helpful to seekers of health and fitness are C (available in supplements and fruits and vegetables, especially citrus fruits), E (available in wheat germ and wheat germ oil), and B complex (available in supplements such as multiple vitamins and liver tablets).

Weight lifting—a competitive sport in which athletes strive to outdo one another in lifting heavy barbells. The term usually refers to Olympic lifting, but can also refer to power lifting.

Weight training—a form of exercise in which muscle groups are worked individually or in groups against resistance, usually in the form of a weighted barbell or two dumbbells. When the number of repetitions of an exercise is increased, usually in a range of 5 to 12, and then the amount of resistance is increased, usually 5 to 10 pounds, the muscles gradually gain strength and, in men, also increase in size.

Index

Index

Weider Barbell Company, 55
Weights, xii, 70
Williams, Jim, 3
Winning Bodybuilding, 67
Women's weight training, x, xi, 58-59
   routines, 69-70
Workouts, xii, xiii-xiv, 67-72
Wrestlers, 6, 27

Wrestler's bridge, 27, *illus.* 26
Wrist curl, 34, *illus.* 35

Y

York Barbell Company, 55
Young, Doug, 3